Sammy Sosa

by Arlene Bourgeois Molzahn

Reading Consultant:
Dr. Robert Miller
Professor of Special Education
Minnesota State University

CAPSTONE BOOKS

an imprint of Capstone Press
Mankato, Minnesota

Capstone Books are published by Capstone Press
151 Good Counsel Drive, P.O. Box 669, Mankato, Minnesota 56002
http://www.capstone-press.com

Library of Congress Cataloging-in-Publication Data
Molzahn, Arlene Bourgeois.
  Sammy Sosa/by Arlene Bourgeois Molzahn.
  p. cm.—(Sports heroes)
  Includes bibliographical references (p. 45) and index.
  Summary: Presents the life and baseball career of the Dominican-born slugger
who, along with Mark McGwire, in 1998 broke the long-standing record of most home
runs hit in a season.
  ISBN 0-7368-0580-X
  1. Sosa, Sammy, 1968—Juvenile literature. 2. Baseball players—Dominican
Republic—Biography—Juvenile literature. [1. Sosa, Sammy, 1968– 2. Baseball
players.] I. Title. II. Sports heroes (Mankato, Minn.)
  GV865.S59 M64 2001
  796.357'092—dc21
  [B]   00-027414

Editorial Credits
Chuck Miller and Matt Doeden, editors; Timothy Halldin, cover designer and illustrator;
  Heidi Schoof and Kimberly Danger, photo researchers

Photo Credits
Active Images, Inc./Chuck Rydlewski, 16; Steve Swope, 20
Allsport USA/Jonathan Daniel, 4, 7, 25, 32, 36; John Swart, 10; Otto Greule, 30;
  Brian Bahr, 35; Vincent LaForet, 39; Matthew Stockman, 42
Corbis, 40
SportsChrome-USA/Jonathan Kirn, cover; Rob Tringali Jr., 9, 12, 18, 29; Steve
  Wolfman, 15; Tony Tomsic, 22; Scott Cunningham, 26

Table of Contents

CHAPTER 1

Chasing
Roger Maris

It was September 13, 1998, at Wrigley Field in Chicago. The Chicago Cubs were playing the Milwaukee Brewers. Cubs' outfielder Sammy Sosa had already hit 60 home runs that season. Sammy needed one more home run to tie Roger Maris's record. Maris hit 61 home runs in 1961. A second home run would break the record. Mark McGwire of the St. Louis Cardinals had broken the record a few days earlier. McGwire had hit 62 home runs so far that season.

Thousands of fans gathered to watch Sammy Sosa on September 13, 1998.

Sammy came up to bat in the fifth inning. Brewers' pitcher Bronswell Patrick threw him a strike. Sammy swung at the pitch and sent the ball flying 480 feet (146 meters). The ball landed on the street behind Wrigley Field's left field fence. Sammy rounded the bases as the fans cheered.

But the game was not over. The Cubs were one run behind the Brewers in the ninth inning. Sammy came up to bat again. With a 2-1 count, Brewers' pitcher Eric Plunk threw a fastball over the plate. Sammy took a powerful swing at the ball. Again, he hit the ball 480 feet over the left field bleachers. It was his 62nd home run. He had tied McGwire in the home-run race.

After Sammy reached home plate, the crowd stood and began shouting his name. People also shouted "MVP-MVP." The crowd believed Sammy should be voted the National League's Most Valuable Player. Sammy came out of the dugout three times to tip his hat. After six

---

Sammy's 62nd home run sent the Cubs and Brewers into extra innings. The Cubs later won 11-10.

minutes, the crowd finally stopped clapping and shouting so the game could go on.

The Cubs won the game by a score of 11-10 in the 10th inning. After the game, the Cubs' players carried Sammy off the field on their shoulders.

About Sammy Sosa

Sammy Sosa is an outfielder for the Chicago Cubs. He has been a major league player since 1989. Today, Sammy is one of the best hitters in baseball. He also is one of the best known athletes in North America.

Sammy is successful off the baseball field as well. He grew up very poor in his home country of the Dominican Republic. But today, Sammy earns millions of dollars by playing baseball and through endorsements. Sammy earns endorsement money for appearing in product advertisements. He appears in commercials for companies such as McDonald's. Sammy gives some of the money he earns to the people of the Dominican Republic. He is a hero to many of the people there.

Sammy Sosa

Major League Batting Statistics

Year	Team	Games	Avg	HR	RBI
1989	Tex/CWS	58	.257	4	13
1990	CWS	153	.233	15	70
1991	CWS	116	.203	10	33
1992	ChC	67	.260	8	25
1993	ChC	159	.261	33	93
1994	ChC	105	.300	25	70
1995	ChC	144	.268	36	119
1996	ChC	124	.273	40	100
1997	ChC	162	.251	36	119
1998	ChC	159	.308	66	158
1999	ChC	162	.288	63	141
Total		1,409	.267	336	941

CHAPTER 2

The Early Years

Sammy Sosa was born November 12, 1968, near San Pedro de Macoris, Dominican Republic. This country is on the island of Hispaniola. Hispaniola is the second largest island in a group of islands called the West Indies.

Sammy's parents were Juan and Lucrecia. Juan worked on a farm. Lucrecia took care of Sammy, his four brothers, and two sisters.

Growing up Poor

The Sosa family was poor. They could afford only a two-room house. Sammy and some of his brothers had to sleep on the floor. Juan and Lucrecia were religious people. They taught

Sammy was born November 12, 1968.

Sammy always had great athletic ability.

their children to believe in God. Lucrecia believed prayers would get her family through hard times.

Sammy's father died when Sammy was 6 years old. Sammy's mother then had to begin working outside the home to support the family. She brought food to people who worked in factories near the Sosa home. Lucrecia did not make much money. Sammy and his brothers also worked. They took any job they could get. They shined shoes, sold oranges, washed cars, and cleaned yards. They gave all of the money they earned to their mother. Lucrecia used their earnings to buy food for the family.

When Sammy was 12, a man named Bill Chase came to San Pedro de Macoris. Chase was from the United States. He came to the Dominican Republic to open three shoe factories. Chase liked Sammy and his brother Juan. He gave the brothers jobs running errands and shining shoes. The boys attended school in the mornings and worked in the shoe factory in the afternoons.

Some of the workers in the shoe factory were from the United States. These workers spoke English. Sammy and Juan spoke only Spanish. The boys learned to speak some English while working at the factory.

Discovering Baseball
Sammy's older brother Luis liked to play baseball. Luis saw that Sammy had athletic

ability. He convinced Sammy to try playing baseball. Sammy quickly took an interest in this sport. His athletic ability made him a good player.

The Dominican Republic had no Little League programs. The country had few baseball parks. Sammy and his friends played in the streets. They rolled up a sock and taped it together for a baseball. They used a stick for a bat. The children did not have baseball gloves. Instead, they used milk cartons that were cut in half. Sammy and his friends played baseball whenever they could.

At age 14, Sammy began playing organized baseball in the Dominican Republic. Sammy could hit a baseball a long way. But he often swung at bad pitches. He sometimes swung too hard. Sammy also could throw a baseball very fast. But he threw wildly. His throws from the outfield sometimes went over the backstop into the crowd. Despite his wild play, Sammy's baseball talent was obvious.

Sammy has played organized baseball since he was 14 years old.

Professional Dreams

One day, Bill Chase watched Sammy play. Chase bought an expensive baseball glove on his next trip to the United States. Chase gave Sammy the glove when he returned to the Dominican Republic.

Sammy began working harder on his baseball skills. He knew that good players could play professionally in the United States. Many players from the Dominican Republic had made it to the major leagues.

Sammy's goal became to play major league baseball in the United States. Sammy knew his family would no longer be poor if he made it to the major leagues.

Sammy's baseball talent was obvious to those who saw him play.

CHAPTER 3

Learning the Game

A scout from the Philadelphia Phillies saw Sammy play when he was only 15 years old. The scout saw Sammy's natural ability and signed him to a contract. But the contract was not legal. Major league players must be at least 16 to sign a contract.

A baseball scout named Omar Minaya heard about Sammy after he turned 16. Minaya worked as a minor league coach for the Texas Rangers. In 1985, Minaya traveled to the Dominican Republic. He arranged to meet with Sammy in the city of Puerto Plata.

Sammy dreamed of someday playing in the major leagues while he lived in the Dominican Republic.

Sammy is Discovered

Sammy borrowed a baseball uniform from a friend and took a bus to meet Minaya. Four hours later, Sammy arrived in the city of Puerto Plata. Minaya was surprised when he saw Sammy. The young player was nearly 6 feet (1.8 meters) tall but weighed only 160 pounds (73 kilograms). He was wearing a pair of old pants. His baseball jersey was faded and had holes under the arms. Even Sammy's shoes had holes in them.

Sammy worked out for Minaya. Minaya immediately noticed the speed with which Sammy swung the bat. He saw that Sammy had a strong throwing arm and a great desire to play. Minaya believed that Sammy could play in the major leagues if he had the right coaching.

Minaya talked to Sammy and his family. He asked Sammy to sign a contract. Minaya told Sammy that the Texas Rangers would sign him as an undrafted free agent. On July 30, 1985,

Baseball scouts noticed Sammy's great bat speed.

A HERO'S HERO

Roberto Clemente

Sammy's hero was a baseball player named Roberto Clemente. Clemente was a native of Puerto Rico. This island is near the Dominican Republic. Clemente was an outfielder for the Pittsburgh Pirates in the early 1970s.

In 1972, Puerto Rico had a major earthquake. Clemente gave money and food to help the people there. He then boarded an airplane to bring supplies to Puerto Rico. The plane crashed into the ocean. Clemente died in the crash.

Sammy respected Clemente as a baseball player and as a person. Sammy wanted to be like Clemente. Today, he wears uniform number 21 in honor of Clemente. Clemente wore number 21 for the Pirates.

Sammy signed a contract to play baseball for the Rangers in the 1986 season. He agreed to a $3,500 signing bonus. He gave the money to his mother. She used some of the money to buy a van for the family.

Sammy Comes to the United States

In January 1986, scouts from the Rangers came to see Sammy in San Pedro de Macoris. They found him selling oranges on a street corner in the city. He was still working hard to make money for his family.

The scouts told Sammy that he would play on a rookie team in the Gulf Coast League. Sammy took a few belongings and the baseball glove Chase had given him. His mother cried when he left on the plane for Florida. Lucrecia knew that her son spoke little English. She also knew that he would put great pressure on himself to succeed.

Life in the United States was difficult for Sammy. The few words of English he knew were not helpful. Even simple things such as ordering food in a restaurant were difficult for him. Sammy would listen to what the other players ordered. He would then order the same thing. He sometimes did not know what kind of food he was ordering.

Sammy met some Puerto Rican baseball players who spoke both English and Spanish. These players helped Sammy improve his English. They also let him live with them. They split the rent and other bills. Sammy sent most of the money left after expenses home to his family in the Dominican Republic.

Sammy has always put a great deal of pressure on himself to succeed.

CHAPTER 4

Professional Baseball

Sammy began his professional baseball career in the spring of 1986. He first played in Sarasota, Florida. He had a promising rookie year. Sammy led the Gulf Coast League in doubles with 19. He also led the league in total bases with 96.

In 1987, Sammy moved up to the Class A League. He played for Gastonia, Georgia, in the South Atlantic League. Sammy's skills continued to improve. His batting average that season was .279. He also had 59 Runs Batted

Sammy has achieved his goal of becoming a major league baseball player.

In (RBIs). He was named to the South Atlantic All-Star team. But Sammy still needed to improve some of his skills. During the season, Sammy struck out 123 times and made 17 outfield errors.

Class A baseball players do not make much money. But Sammy continued to save as much as he could to send home to his family. During this time, Sammy often was homesick. He was not sure that he would ever become good enough to play in the majors.

Sammy played Class A ball again in 1988. The Rangers moved him to Port Charlotte, Florida, in the Florida State League. Sammy struggled that year. He was not patient enough at the plate. He often swung at pitches far outside of the strike zone. His batting average dipped to .229. But he still showed some promise. His coaches were impressed by his speed and power.

Sammy moved up to Class AA baseball in the Texas League in 1989. He played in Tulsa, Oklahoma. After 66 games, his batting

Sammy prepared for his major league career during his years in the minor leagues.

average was near .300. He had seven home runs and had driven in 31 runs. Sammy made fewer mistakes in the outfield. He also showed better control at the plate.

In June 1989, Sammy received a call from the Rangers. They wanted him to report to the major league team. Sammy was about to reach

his goal. He was going to become a major league baseball player.

The Major Leagues
On June 16, 1989, Sammy played his first game with the Rangers. The Rangers were playing the New York Yankees. Sammy got two hits in four times at bat. He hit his first major league home run five days later against the Boston Red Sox. But Sammy's success did not last long. He struggled at the plate and in the field. After 25 games, the Rangers sent him back to the minor leagues.

By the end of July, the Texas Rangers had given up on Sammy. On July 29, 1989, the Rangers traded Sammy to the Chicago White Sox.

The Chicago White Sox sent Sammy to their Class AAA team in Vancouver, British Columbia, Canada. Sammy had to learn to live in yet another country. But the move was good for him. The coaches told Sammy he was trying too hard. Sammy began to relax on the field. In just 49 times at bat, he recorded 18 hits, five RBIs, and one home run. His batting average

In 1989, the Texas Rangers traded Sammy to the Chicago White Sox.

Sammy played parts of three seasons for the White Sox.

was .367. The White Sox liked the way Sammy was playing. They asked him to join their team in Chicago.

On August 22, 1989, Sammy played his first game with the White Sox. He continued to play for the White Sox in the 1990 and 1991 seasons. He showed the ability to make good plays at times. But he also continued to make mistakes at the plate and in the field.

Sammy Becomes a Cub

The White Sox traded Sammy to the Chicago Cubs before the 1992 baseball season. Sammy suffered several injuries during his first year with the Cubs. In early June, Sammy was hit by a pitch that broke a bone in his right hand. He could not play for more than a month. In early August, Sammy hit a ball off his left ankle. Sammy could not play for the rest of the season.

In 1993, Sammy finished the year with a .261 batting average and 93 RBIs. Sammy also became the first 30–30 player in Cubs history. He did this by hitting 33 home runs and stealing 36 bases.

Sammy began the 1994 season strong. He was batting .300 with 25 home runs and 70 RBIs. But the season ended early. The last game was played on August 11. A strike by the players then ended the season. The players did not think the team owners were treating them fairly.

The Cubs were pleased with Sammy's play. They offered him a contract for the 1995 season. The contract would pay Sammy more than $4 million. Sammy was happy. He would finally be able to help his family as much as he wanted.

Success with the Cubs

In 1995, Sammy recorded another 30–30 season. He hit 36 home runs and stole 34 bases. Sammy also had 119 RBIs. After the 1995 season, the Cubs offered Sammy a two-year contract worth more than $10 million.

In 1996, Sammy was playing well. He had hit 40 home runs and had driven in 100 runs. But on August 20, he was hit with an inside pitch. The pitch broke a bone in his right hand. Another season ended early for Sammy.

Sammy struggled after the injury to his hand. In 1997, Sammy hit 36 home runs. But his batting average dipped to .251. He led the National League in strikeouts with 174.

Sammy had another slow start in 1998. But he soon recovered. Sammy hit 20 home runs during the month of June. This number was a record for the most home runs in one month.

Mark McGwire also was hitting home runs at a record-breaking pace. Sammy and

Both Sammy and Mark McGwire broke Roger Maris's home-run record in 1998.

McGwire took turns leading the home-run race that season. Both players broke the record. McGwire ended the season with 70 home runs. Sammy finished with 66 home runs.

Sammy's success in 1998 helped the Cubs make the National League playoffs. But they lost to the Atlanta Braves in the first round. After the season, Sammy was named the National League's Most Valuable Player.

CHAPTER 5

Sammy Sosa Today

In 1999, Sammy and McGwire began another home-run race. Sammy hit his 60th home run on September 18 against the Milwaukee Brewers. He became the first player in major league history to hit 60 home runs two years in a row.

Sammy Sosa ended the season with 63 home runs. He also had 141 RBIs and a .288 average. But McGwire again won the home-run race. McGwire finished the season with 65 home runs. Many people believed Sammy should

Sammy hit 63 home runs in 1999.

win another MVP award. But the Cubs had a poor record in 1999. The MVP award usually goes to a player on a winning team. Chipper Jones of the Braves won the award instead. Sammy did not even finish among the top five.

Sammy's Family

Today, Sammy is married and has his own family. He and his wife, Sonia, have four children. The children are Keysha, Kenia, Sammy Jr., and Michael.

The Sosa family lives in Chicago during the baseball season. Sonia and the children cheer Sammy on at the Cubs' home games. During the winter, Sammy and his family spend time in the Dominican Republic.

Sammy's mother still lives in the Dominican Republic. But she now lives in a nice home and no longer has to worry about money. Lucrecia watches Sammy play baseball on TV. Sammy remembers his mother while he plays. After

Sammy remains close with his mother, Lucrecia.

In December 1997, Sammy went on a "Sammy Claus" tour in the United States.

each home run, Sammy touches his heart and blows a kiss to the camera for Lucrecia.

Helping People in Need

Sammy did not forget about the people of the Dominican Republic. In 1996, he built a shopping center in his hometown of San Pedro de Macoris. This shopping center included business offices, a medical center, and small shops. Sammy's sisters own a small store and a hair salon there. The shopping center is named Plaza 30–30 in honor of Sammy's two 30–30 seasons with the Cubs. The shopping center provides jobs for many of the people in the area.

Sammy also helps the children of the Dominican Republic. He has given 250 computers to schools there. Sammy also started a baseball school for poor boys in the country. The boys live at the school. They learn about baseball and other subjects. Sammy and the school provide the boys with food and baseball equipment. Sammy is a hero to many people in the Dominican Republic for his success and his efforts to help.

Sammy also helps children in the United States. Sammy gives away 50 tickets for every Sunday game the Cubs play at home. He gives these tickets to children who cannot afford them. He calls these days "Sammy's Super Sundays for Cubs." In December 1997, Sammy went on a "Sammy Claus" tour to seven cities in the United States. He dressed as Santa Claus and gave more than 7,000 gifts to children in hospitals and schools.

Career Highlights

1968—Sammy is born on November 12 near San Pedro de Macoris, Dominican Republic.

1985—Sammy signs a professional contract with the Texas Rangers.

1986—Sammy begins his professional baseball career in Sarasota, Florida.

1989—Sammy plays for the Texas Rangers in his first major league game. Later that year, he is traded to the Chicago White Sox.

1992—The White Sox trade Sammy to the Chicago Cubs.

1993—Sammy becomes first Cubs' player ever to hit 30 home runs and steal 30 bases in one season.

1995—Sammy plays in his first All-Star game.

1996—On June 5, Sammy hits 3 home runs in one game.

1997—On August 20, Sammy records his 1,000th major league hit.

1998—On July 27, Sammy hits his first grand slam home run. He finishes the season with 66 home runs and wins the National League MVP award.

1999—Sammy becomes the first player to hit 60 home runs two seasons in a row.

Words to Know

bonus (BOH-nuhss)—a sum of money paid to a player for signing a contract

contract (KON-trakt)—an agreement between an owner and a player; contracts determine players' salaries.

endorse (en-DORSS)—to sponsor a product by appearing in advertisements

free agent (FREE AY-juhnt)—a player who is free to sign with any team

professional (pruh-FESH-uh-nuhl)—someone who is paid to participate in a sport

rookie (RUK-ee)—a first-year player

strike (STRIKE)—to refuse to work until a set of demands are met

To Learn More

Dougherty, Terri. *Sammy Sosa.* Jam Session. Minneapolis: Abdo, 1999.

Maclean, Caleb. *Sammy Sosa, Cubs Clubber.* Sports Stars. New York: Children's Press, 1999.

Powell, Phelan. *Mark McGwire.* Sports Heroes. Mankato, Minn.: Capstone Books, 2001.

Romero, Maritza. *Roberto Clemente: Baseball Hall of Famer.* Great Hispanics of Our Time. New York: PowerKids Press, 1997.

Useful Addresses

Major League Baseball
Office of the Commissioner of Baseball
245 Park Avenue, 31st Floor
New York, NY 10167

National Baseball Hall of Fame
    and Museum
25 Main Street
P.O. Box 590
Cooperstown, NY 13326

Sammy Sosa
c/o Chicago Cubs
1060 West Addison Street
Chicago, IL 60613-4397

Internet Sites

Chicago Cubs
http://www.chicagocubs.com

CNN/SI—Sammy Sosa
http://sportsillustrated.cnn.com/baseball/mlb/ml/
   players/4344/index.html

ESPN.com—Sammy Sosa
http://espn.go.com/mlb/profiles/profile/4344.html

Major League Baseball
http://www.majorleaguebaseball.com

Index